GOOD, BETTER, BEST

THE STORY OF MARY AND MARTHA

By Marilyn Lashbrook

Illustrated by Stephanie McFetridge Britt

ME TOO!
B O O K S

ROPER PRESS, INC.
DALLAS, TEXAS

"Good, Better, Best" will motivate your preschooler to slow down and listen to God's Word. Time with Jesus is one part of the day none of us should miss.

On the first reading, pause and allow your child to respond to the statement, "Count to three." After several readings, pause and allow your child to say the words in italics, giving a clue when needed.

Children have great memories. Ask your child to remind you to read him a Bible verse and pray with him at a given time each day (before nap, after sister leaves for school). Reward your child with a sticker for reminding you.

WS ES

Library of Congress Catalog Card Number: 94-066483
ISBN 0-86606-452-4

Art Direction and design by
    Chris Schechner Graphic Design

GOOD, BETTER, BEST

THE STORY OF MARY AND MARTHA

By Marilyn Lashbrook

Illustrated by Stephanie McFetridge Britt

Taken from Luke 10

ME TOO! BOOKS

Count to three. *One, two, three. . .* Jesus had three special friends.

Mary and Martha were sisters. Lazarus was their brother.

Jesus came to the city of Bethany.
He came to see His three friends.

Martha invited Jesus and His followers to come for dinner.
Martha loved to cook for people.
Some people are good cooks.
Some people are better cooks.
Martha wanted to be the best cook of all.

One, two, three. Good, better, best.

Mary and Martha had a lot of cooking to do. They had a lot of cleaning to do. They worked until the house was clean.

Do you think Martha was happy? No.

They worked until the house was cleaner.

Now do you think Martha was happy? No.

They worked and worked until the house was the cleanest house in town. Still Martha was not happy. Everything had to be perfect.

One, two, three. Clean, cleaner, cleanest.

The sisters were working hard.
Then Jesus came. Martha barely noticed.

But Mary rushed to see Him. She forgot about the cooking and cleaning. All she wanted to do was listen to Jesus.

Mary sat quietly on the floor in front of Jesus. She listened carefully to every word He said.

Mary didn't see Jesus very often. Now that He was in her home, she wanted to spend every minute learning from Him.

Mary was happy to know Jesus. She was happier when He was in her home.
But she was happiest when He was telling her about God.

One, two, three. Happy, happier, happiest.

Martha rushed here and there all by herself.
She hurried to finish the decorating.
She ran to check the stove.
She scurried to set the table.
She was busy, busier, busiest of all.

One, two, three. Busy, busier, busiest.

Martha waited for Mary to help her, but Mary did not come back.

At first, Martha was a little angry.
After a while, she was angrier.
She fussed and fumed.
She steamed and stormed.
And when she was the angriest she could be, she decided to speak up.

One, two, three. Angry, angrier, angriest.

Martha went to Jesus.

"Tell Mary to help me!" she demanded.

"She left me to do all the work!"

Jesus understood Martha's feelings. He knew
she wanted to have a nice dinner for Him.

Count to three. *One, two, three.* . . Jesus had three special friends.

He wanted time with His friends more than He wanted a fancy dinner.

Soon Jesus would have to leave. Then it would be too late to spend time together.

"Martha, Martha, you are worried about so many things." Jesus said. "Mary has chosen the better thing."

Working is good.
Spending time learning about God is better.
Being with Jesus is best of all.

One, two, three. Good, better, best.

Some things can wait.

Some things can't.

Martha rushed around the house,
Too busy for the Lord.
But Mary sat at Jesus' feet,
And listened to His Word.

Oh to be like Mary,
and near to Jesus stay,
To listen to His precious Word,
And talk to Him each day.

ME TOO!
B O O K S

For Ages 2-5

SOMEONE TO LOVE
THE STORY OF CREATION

TWO BY TWO
THE STORY OF NOAH'S FAITH

"I DON'T WANT TO"
THE STORY OF JONAH

"I MAY BE LITTLE"
THE STORY OF DAVID'S GROWTH

"I'LL PRAY ANYWAY"
THE STORY OF DANIEL

WHO NEEDS A BOAT?
THE STORY OF MOSES

"GET LOST LITTLE BROTHER"
THE STORY OF JOSEPH

THE WALL THAT DID NOT FALL
THE STORY OF RAHAB'S FAITH

NO TREE FOR CHRISTMAS
THE STORY OF JESUS' BIRTH

"NOW I SEE"
THE STORY OF THE MAN BORN BLIND

DON'T ROCK THE BOAT!
THE STORY OF THE MIRACULOUS CATCH

OUT ON A LIMB
THE STORY OF ZACCHAEUS

SOWING AND GROWING
THE PARABLE OF THE SOWER AND THE SOILS

DON'T STOP . . . FILL EVERY POT
THE STORY OF THE WIDOW'S OIL

GOOD, BETTER, BEST
THE STORY OF MARY AND MARTHA

GOD'S HAPPY HELPERS
THE STORY OF TABITHA AND FRIENDS

ME TOO!
R E A D E R S

For Ages 5-8

IT'S NOT MY FAULT
MAN'S BIG MISTAKE

GOD, PLEASE SEND FIRE!
ELIJAH AND THE PROPHETS OF BAAL

TOO BAD, AHAB!
NABOTH'S VINEYARD

THE WEAK STRONGMAN
SAMSON

NOTHING TO FEAR
JESUS WALKS ON WATER

THE BEST DAY EVER
THE STORY OF JESUS

THE GREAT SHAKE-UP
MIRACLES IN PHILIPPI

TWO LADS AND A DAD
THE PRODIGAL SON

Available at your local bookstore or from:
Roper Press
4737-A Gretna
Dallas, Texas 75207
1-800-284-0158